Boo Boo Laroo Follows the Clue

WRITTEN BY
DR. PEGGY MCCOLL

ILLUSTRATED BY
JOEL CHRISTOPHER PAYNE

Published by:
Hasmark Publishing International
www.hasmarkpublishing.com

Copyright © 2025 Peggy McColl
First Edition

All Rights Reserved. No part of this book may be reproduced or transmitted in any form or by any means, electronic or mechanical, including photocopying, recording or by any information storage and retrieval system, without written permission from the author, except for the inclusion of brief quotations in a review.

Disclaimer:
This book is designed to provide information and motivation to our readers. It is sold with the understanding that the publisher is not engaged to render any type of psychological, legal, or any other kind of professional advice. The content of each article is the sole expression and opinion of its author, and not necessarily that of the publisher. No warranties or guarantees are expressed or implied by the publisher's choice to include any of the content in this volume. Neither the publisher nor the individual author(s) shall be liable for any physical, psycho- logical, emotional, financial, or commercial damages, including, but not limited to, special, incidental, consequential or other damages. Our views and rights are the same: You are responsible for your own choices, actions, and results.

Permission should be addressed in writing to Peggy McColl at Peggy@PeggyMcColl.com.

Interior Layout: Amit Dey [amit@hasmarkpublishing.com]

Illustrations & Cover Design: Joel Christopher Payne

ISBN 13: 978-1-77482-345-3
ISBN 10: 1-77482-345-4

DEDICATION

To my beautiful granddaughter,

Aria Mae

Boo Boo Laroo leapt out of her bed, with wild messy curls and an idea in her head.

She looked under tables, she looked in her bed, she peeked in the closet and stood on her head!

NO SHOE ON THE STAIRS, NO SHOE IN THE LOO — THEN BOO BOO LAROO FOUND A CURIOUS CLUE.

"A TRAIL!" BOO BOO GASPED. "THERE'S MORE I MUST DO — I THINK IT MIGHT LEAD TO MY RUNAWAYSHOE!"

She tiptoed through crafts, she tiptoed through glue, past markers and glitter and paintings she knew.

EACH LITTLE MESS GAVE HER SOMETHING TO SPY —
EACH ONE A SPARKLE THAT CAUGHT HER BRIGHT EYE!

THE TRAIL TWISTED
RIGHT WHERE THE WHITE DAISIES GROW.

AND TUCKED IN A BASKET
(WITH GLITTER AND GLUE)...

THERE IT WAS — SHINING! HER LOST, FAVORITE SHOE!

BOO BOO LAROO SLIPPED HER FOOT IN WITH GLEE, SHE TWIRLED AND DANCED LIKE A BUMBLEBEE!

**SHE SMILED AND SHE SHOUTED, "WOO-HOO, I FOUND YOU!"
THAT'S WHAT CAN HAPPEN WHEN YOU FOLLOW A CLUE!**

THE END

ABOUT THE AUTHOR

Dr. Peggy McColl is a New York Times Bestselling Author, passionate storyteller, and loving grandmother who has dedicated her life to inspiring both young and old through the power of words. With more than two decades of experience writing transformational books for adults, Peggy now brings her heartfelt wisdom and creativity to the world of children's literature.

Boo Boo Laroo Follows The Clue was inspired by her deep love for her granddaughter, Aria, and her desire to create meaningful, joy-filled stories that encourage curiosity, wonder, and connection. The very first time Peggy read Boo Boo Laroo Follows The Clue to Aria, her granddaughter looked up with wide eyes and one simple request: "Again." And so, they read it again. And again. And again.

That moment — the pure joy of a child wanting more — became one of the most meaningful experiences in Peggy's life as an author. It was the greatest compliment she could ever receive.

When she's not writing, Peggy loves spending time with her family—including her beloved grandchildren, James and Aria—soaking in nature, and dreaming up magical stories that spark imagination and fill hearts. She believes stories not only entertain, but also plant powerful seeds of possibility in the hearts of children everywhere.

To learn more about Peggy and her work, visit PeggyMcColl.com